Marigram

POEMS BY

VIVIAN FAITH PRESCOTT

GLASS LYRE PRESS

Copyright © 2023 Vivian Faith Prescott
Paperback ISBN: 979-8-9885737-2-2

All rights reserved: Except for the purpose of quoting brief passages for review, no part of this book may be reproduced or transmitted in any form or by any means, electronic or mechanical, including photocopying, recording, or by any information storage and retrieval system, without permission in writing from the publisher.

Design & Layout: Steven Asmussen
Cover Art: "Tide Pooling" by Evon Zerbetz https://www.evonzerbetz.com/

Glass Lyre Press, LLC
P.O. Box 2693
Glenview, IL 60025
www.GlassLyrePress.com

Marigram

To my father,
Mickey of Mickey's Fishcamp,
recorder of weather, fishing, and stories.

Marigram: A graphic record of the tide levels at a particular coastal station.

Contents

Fishcamp Kismet	1
Reference Station	3
Oceanic	4
Kymatology: How to or *How Not to* Ride the Waves	5
Siedde	7
Map of Dogs	8
Hydrographic	10
The Driving Force	12
Like Dreams to a Sleeper	13
The Cabin Aubade	14
The Inside Passage	15
Goldeneye Morning	16
In the creaking and noises, an old conversation	17
Intertidal	18
Drift Current	19
Outbreaking	20
Coriolis Force	21
Listening Station	22
Overlooking	23
Foraging Zone	24
Seawall	26
Lunicurrent	27
Local Geology	28
Storm at Mickey's Fishcamp	30
Retroflection	31
From the Body that is an Ocean	33
Acknowledgements	35
About the Author	37

Fishcamp Kismet

The small dead spider in my bedsheets
      is shaken out over my porch railing

at the edge of the sea.

Atop my seawall, a wild
strawberry plant from the Stikine River

blooms
little white flowers out of the skull

of a baby humpback whale.

On the beach below my fishcamp,
the wing bones of an eagle stretch out,

flesh-bare, as if ready to catch an updraft.

In the bluedark, a mouse falls from the sky
and thuds against my window.

These startles,
are a bit like a martin darting

into the crevasse in the seawall,
and sometimes they linger as long

as a hummingbird drinks nectar from
a bleeding heart.

Before these moments disappear,
      I often think—I will remember

how this wisp of eagle down swayfalls
like snow

onto my open palm. And then I don't.

There is a thick curtain
like old-man's-beard-moss

hanging from hemlocks, separating
my world from that other

shadowy dirt road,

that sweeps aside   again and   again,
without my having to draw back the strands.

Often it brushes away when
the weight of my footfalls crush

a raven's hat—the limpet—
and burst open popweed bladders.

Call me lucky, if you will—the old seawall

is the only thing protecting me now
    from the rush of tide,

and the strawberries
are ripening in the eye sockets of a whale.

Reference Station

My deep-set memory of salmonberries
sweet on the tongue,

of leaves caught in my hair, of a grandchild
swinging a plastic berry bucket,

is now a pale wound. I was hoping for
sun-filled and berried days,

but skies promise rain again and I haven't even
hung the hammock yet.

A season like this would have us believing
in an apocalypse—

a shoreline littered with sea mammals, a virus,
a salmon fishing closure.

My wish-stone offerings tucked into the cracks
of my seawall now seem futile.

The universe will just sweep them out again
on the next high tide.

Oceanic

Frost forms ancient patterns in puddles,
brown leaves curl from cold on the thin alder.

This cabin perches like a blinking moon
atop our seawall. Moonlight pools atop sea,

clings like glitter to porch rails and stone steps,
nightfall seeps through cabin walls.

Awakening at midnight with waves of tide
glimmering on the ceiling, the bay's moonlight

scatters across my bed and I pull covers down
and let sealight ripple on skin,

and like a small feather adrift,
I revel in shimmering waves of light,

until I sink into the pillow of sea, falling
into that deep trough, into the dream of dark brine.

Kymatology: How to or *How Not to* Ride the Waves

1.   Ride like my Tlingit/Sámi/Filipino/Hawaiian grade-school grandsons in the Sitka surf. bobbing like seals. in their wet suits. on boogie boards. in November.

2.   Ride like a seasickness mirage—commercial fishing offshore in the Gulf of Alaska. daughter sees brown bear spirits surfing the waves. offshore of Lituya Bay. in oral traditions—brown bear spirits live there.

3.   Ride like 8-foot chop on the Stikine River flats—riding home with drunk river rats. hanging onto the runabout's dash. seats not bolted in. sliding to the stern. drunk men. me.

4.   Ride the grief of another cousin, friend, fisherman, drowned. found tangled in a fishing boat's rigging. found floating. found beneath a toppled canoe. stuck under a dock. on an icefloe. along a beach. or not found at all.

5.   Ride like my dream when I was a salmon. floating. floating, in a school of fish. reach to touch them. feel their fins and bodies swim by me. poet friend is standing on the beach, telling the Salmon Boy story, calling us home. home.

6.   Ride like Uncle Howard through the story he told my kids— the time he and his son rode a mega-tsunami in his fishing boat over Cenotaph Island in Lituya Bay. highest wave ever recorded. hope like that. he said. ride your life like that.

7.   Ride like the Man-of-Lit.uaa who shakes his blanket and sends waves knocking around Lituya Bay. my children's ancestral homeland. offer him/sea monster some tobacco. offer a lock of your hair when entering the bay.

8.   Ride like a dance robe— Chaas' Koowu Tlaa—Mother-of-Humpy-Tail weaves a raven's tail robe—seismograph and mountains carved by a wave. waves woven with mountain goat hair. sea otter fur. put on the robe and dance the wave.

9.   Daughter, ride the asphalt waves rolling over the Alaska highway—megathrust earthquake. you drove through. sonic boom. car shaking. drive faster. largest inland quake in 150 years. 7.9. rippling ocean. 4 minutes in an apocalyptic movie, you say.

10.   Ride like a freakish July storm. waves crashing into my seawall at fishcamp. wash sea spray from my windows. ride a year with storms. ride a year with no salmon. ride thoughts of the nearby glacier. melting.

11.   Ride the uplift and subsurface rupture: My cousin Jerry, working the docks in Valdez, Alaska in 1964 when a tsunami of mud and sea swept him away. 9.2 earthquake. underwater landslide. water retreated from shore. swept back in. smashed a freighter. killed longshoremen. my cousin. and children. washed away the waterfront.

12.   Ride November, ride spirits, ride chop, ride grief, ride dreams. ride toward home and ride away from home. ride taboos and dancing. ride asphalt and storms. ride the apocalypse. never still. ride the wind. ride the pull of the moon. ride our energy passing through this world. hang on. every one of us—ride our stories.

*Kymatology: the science of waves and wave motion.

Siedde

"A strong Sámi identity enhances the mental well-being of Sámi"
—Klemetti Näkkäläjärvi

Rocky shoreline, bend of bay, seawall
built of boulders and stone stairs

leading up to my cabin. It was fair weather
and calm seas all year

so we picked berries through summer,
always a bucket of blueberries, stained lips,

bellies full of fish and now there's a deer
packed in the freezer.

The spirit of the ancients visit us here too—
a kingfisher sits on the porch railing,

a hawk circles the beach, owls have been
hooting up these fall nights in nearby woods,

and the ravens and crows gather up
our mornings. Living near the seidde,

a gathering place for resting spirits in transition—
    remove your hat,
    respect the quiet,
    know the sacred songs.

Let me repay the spirits for our gifts—
offer our bounty to others, leave an offering
of a bird-shaped stone.

Map of Dogs

"Where you find a dog's bones, man might not be far behind."
       —Anthropologist

Our island's shapeline resembles a snow goose flying to the river flats
and I live in the crook of the goose's neck with two border collies,

Oscar and Kéet. I am the benchmark here, the permanent material
object, a marked point unto myself, and yet,

I traverse landmarks of neighbors by bend of road, line of crabapple
and meander of seawall. Forestry map, geological map, line map,

flood map, dog map—Patsy, Kiera, Baily, Finn, Scout and Daisy,
canine coordinates I walk to every morning. Dogs I've followed,

tossed a stick for, called up, even shooed away. If I could, I'd walk
beyond this map's margins, though, head east toward the mainland

to Bear Toe Cave, a hollow holding bear's metacarpal, raven's radius.
I'd find a spear point, bone awl, shell beads, and a tiny femur—

the oldest dog remains found in North America. Both dog
and human with a shared diet of seal, whale, and salmon.

When the band of ice melted, who led or followed whom to the cave?
And as the night-fire danced on stone, loyal companion,

a palm pressed atop your head, you curled together for warmth.
And perhaps it was that night or another when you followed

the well-traveled map of time to this moment, ten thousand years later,
and here I am charting our intersection: Dog and human

sitting on my porch next to the sea, and me scratching the dog's chin—
Good dog. Good. Dog.

Hydrographic

How is it that I found this universe in proximity
to a shoreline with edge waves nudging me to sleep at night.

> *Night sleeps in waves, nudging me nearer*
> *to the universe's shoreline.*

How is it that my blood's salinity is this poetic.
The pull of the moon pulls words from me each morning.

> *The morning pulls the poetic moon from me,*
> *pooling my blood's salinity into words.*

I call her Ocean, nothing extravagant, but say her name
out loud, bid her goodnight each night.

> *Night bids goodnight out loud, saying her name:*
> *"Ocean, Ocean."*

Each day I walk the zone between mean high and low water,
searching for the right rhythm and line.

> *The line moves with a rhythm of high*
> *and low water, searching for meaning.*

I pick up remnants of storm washed shells, broken bits of glass.

> *Glass, washed with storm, is a remnant of time.*

The fairy sparks glow in the boat's wake in front of my house—
I imagine diatoms need to dance.

> *Dancing needs to imagine diatoms in the boat's wake,*
> *a house awake and aglow, imagining fairies.*

The flood and glut of rain, an aftermath of squall and snowmelt—
ribbons of the Stikine River in sea-green and brown mud
along the shoreline.

> *The winter shoreline longs for ribbons of river mud*
> *and sea—each spring, flooding with squall and snowmelt.*

The morning's perspectives are tideland dynamic—eagles
bathe, crows and gulls drop clamshells to break them
open for breakfast, a thrush searches the seagrass for insects.

> *I break open. in waves. in words. in high and low water.*
> *in a limpet's shell. in a boat's wake. in a spring flood.*
> *a tideland. I break open.*

The Driving Force

Falling older is not like growing, but a wave
of memories rolling up to press against my seawall.

Ageing tumbles me over stones, over this strip
of sand, blue mussels, and popweed.

There is no refuge from this rain and grayness,
this slack of tide.

What would I trade these years for?

My popular days of driving the meandering
roads of our island?

Me and two other mothers and our toddlers
fleeing the stink of drunken husbands.

Our tart and cranky secrets told amongst
ourselves, while wandering through neighborhoods

in a conversion van. We burned the fuel of days
and sometimes the evenings whenever they turned cruel

from a busted door hinge and an ax-thwacked
car hood. Maybe we felt time pulsing even then.

We surely knew the old stories of freak storms
and tsunami surges that washed over our dirt roads.

Maybe, though we accepted the power of oceans,
swept along with it all, our fates, spinning us around
in the gyre.

Like Dreams to a Sleeper

"For the Sámi, the fire is more than light and warmth: it is a friend…"
    —Emilie DeMant Hatt

Washed to the shoreline, your story seeks
a womb, a sheltering, even a spring fire

as a window to remember fragments
of offerings carried home within us.

But you realize a charm needs a spine,
a drum, a beating heart, and shoulders,

a hand to set wood on flames, open
the eyes in the firewood. This telling

readies spirits to sing and story with us
all night, maybe learn a trick or two,

how to cut off bear's long tail, how to see
the old witch woman, stuck in pitch,

her beetle form flailing on the bright
night's moon.

The Cabin Aubade

Somewhere my dreams are tangled in sheets
and she is still lying beside me.
Somewhere, night is carved with river and sand,

and on the other side of the veil, a cabin is edged
in gold moonlight. In that world, there is another
tender body, another love,

though the same small patch of fireweed still grows
next to the porch and the cottonwood leaves
still turn in the wind.

All night, star girls danced in their own circle,
above us, to flickers of song notes, but now
threads of dawn weave through forest.

Perhaps it was only an ancient longing, stirring hope
as medicine for despair with a dreamfire's snap
and warming of hands.

But not before it caressed love's sheen along her
shoulder, then slipped though the cabin door
without creaking, and ducked out from under

shadows, and walked a pine laden path toward
a breaking sky, toward this day, pink with blushing.

The Inside Passage

"Look down on the sky ocean."
—Aillohas, Sami poet: Nils-Aslak Valkeapaa

This solitude is liquid, a weary stream
tracing distant journeys.

Even the empty fish-cleaning table
is slipping into an echo.

What if time spooled with
the tempo of a melt season

back to our own screaming origins,
how we met this life with eyelids open

about to slide into this psycho ocean,
this warm climate, this inhaled disease.

What is there to offer up
to the gods now—soft apples

and tasteless honeydews
barged up from Seattle,

a spruce root basket woven in this strange year,
or maybe a desk stacked with unfished poems?

All I can focus on lately is adjusting
to new conditions and avoiding predators.

Goldeneye Morning

Ducks float near barnacled shore,
and breeze ripples sea as each wrinkle
moves closer to the faint sun.

This day, though, warm enough
to sit outside sweatered with moments
of sky, white clouds brushing

snow-dusted mountains, is what I need
beneath my tender skin, to fill my
inner archipelago.

I wrap my hands around warm cup,
coffee scent and salted sea, take notice
of Barrow or Common—things my
father taught me—look closer.

Note the triangle head, round white spot
or crescent-shaped behind the bill.
The ducks dip their heads into the sea

hunting for blue mussels and sea stars.
What is it you search for? I say aloud,
straightway, wondering if I am asking
the ducks or asking me.

In the creaking and noises, an old conversation

After Elizabeth Bishop

In the creaking and noises, an old conversation
along the spine of us, like bruising beneath our skin,

making us ache, like wounds left in the dark,
and voices meant for shadows. Old stories—

My father's classmate shot to death by her husband
for sleeping with her lover. The husband lived a long
life on the island.

And another story my dad tells of breaking up a fight
between a prominent couple, pulling the man off the woman.

They stayed married, built a big business.
In the creaking and noises, and old conversation—

the melodrama play, a gun loaded with blanks,
and the blank hitting the actor in his soft belly,

killing him. The shooter, a teenage actor.
These are the old conversations, disappearing

with this generation, each obituary written
in our local paper. A child who once started a fire,

a fish poacher, a drunkard who forced himself
on our island women. These stories end all the same,

with a black and white photo, the bereaved memories
of a favorite fishing hole, or moose hunt,

the list of family, and a sense that we're all survivors,
and the newsprint—cut out as a piece of our tender skin.

*Title and line from poem "The Moose" in Geography by Elizabeth Bishop.

Intertidal

After Linda Hogan

Be like the barnacle that fastens
to the slick boulder, stick to your
intertidal habitat or be the one
who leaps over tide pools.

Be like a frilled dogwinkle
and use your teeth-covered tongue
to suck out barnacle guts, or be its shell
making music on a windchime.

Be like the plate limpet, fill children's
pockets. Resemble a beautiful nipple,
a sombrero, or an Unungan bentwood
hunter's cap.

Be a Yéil Saaxu—a hat for Raven
the trickster. Be all of this.

Drift Current

The poet is asking why
her footprints have filled up with the rising sea.

The poet wants to know
how shadows linger on the hillside all morning.

There she goes—the poet is looking
at the sandflea jumping on her shoe.

Why is it that the poet bothers the universe
with all her questions?

Does she really want to know
why the little neck clam burrows into mud?

Outbreaking

On record, beyond our view,
        is always another apocalypse—
a star is now fading into a galaxy's shadow,

        and the last of an unseen species
is trodden beneath our feet.
        Lately, I can sense

there's an ancient current at the edge
        of myself
and the wind is washing over me

        to clear my thoughts.
Somehow, I need to know if there is
        a pattern to all of this—

I can see a crack in the purest of ice
        and already the last twig
on the Great Earth Tree has snapped

        under the weight of our sorrows.
As this year turns, I'm ready to sing,
        dance, drum, or recite anything

to spook the horsemen, send them fleeing.
        Now hand me the knife
to cute the threads of this woven gloom

so I can let the bright days in again.

Coriolis Force

To you, inhabitants of my cells,
I am still a small rock

teetering on a faultline,
a root fingering out beneath

a thin layer of soil,
I was expected to expect death

to rage into that unknowing space,
to unfasten my skin

from this weeping.
But here I am instead,

a moon-drowned body sitting
on my porch next to the sea,

in the cool night,

still casting faint shadows,
wiping glacier dust from

the soles of my feet.

Listening Station

Not slam of truck doors, moose stomps,
or red chrysanthemum fireworks, or snow

thudding off our roof, but energy waves
across the sea—Hunga Tonga-Hunga Ha'apai,

erupting in plumes of smoke, ash, a storm
of lightning, a tsunami.

Somewhere, it rains pebbles and darkness,
while I am in a river of warm sleep,

cradled between the audible range
of a wave rushing the seawall below

and a pygmy owl on winterbare branch.
Was it an onshore wind shaking my cabin walls

or a sonic boom from a mushroom cloud above
the blue Pacific?—I could not have dreamed that up,

while nestled into the belief of an ocean shared
in the damp night wrapped with breath.

Overlooking

I want to live on like you,
rock-sheltered and etched as a porpoise

or killer whale with my adzework catching rain
and sunlight, lichen-patched,

beside a record of time—dots on a leaning rock wall
noting days and nights in an old winter village.

I want to animate shadows and waves like you
beneath overhanging rock, a canvas

for an image of a face or a paddling canoe.
I want to be ground stone and obsidian flakes,

red pigment binding with pitch, a vantage point
in these uncertain seasons. Oh, to be painted.

Foraging Zone

Stand with a thin fabric of sea lettuce—
        hold it up to the light—
See this beach for the habitat it is.

I am living in this archipelago
        in the land-sea interface,
the marine shoreline, on this old island

among sea stars and black turnstones pecking
        for breakfast among intertidal rocks.
I walk among barnacles and mussels,

not like a black bear crunching shore crabs,
        but a wanderer taking in the wonder
of the sea milkwort and the Lyngbye's sedge.

The world, according to this beach,
        is a parallel universe
with the glow of phones and TV—

All the noise of us.
        Here, I'm the resident vertebrate,
both herbivore and carnivore.

Here, the Seaweed Folk,
        some call them bull-kelp,
rolled up with tide, wash up with tails

ripped from seafloor in yet another storm
        and now rest at my dogs' feet.
I've hollowed bull kelp

to make drinking cups and rattles.
        I've dried them, pickled them,
chopped them to eat.

Now, like deer, bear, and geese, I forage
        and fill my basket
with the goose tongue, beach spinach,

glasswort, traveling across this universe
        in my rubber boots,
like the Old Tide Lady—and look, there's a raven walking this way.

Seawall

Nothing
separates us/me
from the sealion. I catch his breath-scent.

If I don't hear the ocean next to my pillow,
all is not well in the world.

The small stone that I swear was gold,
I stuffed into the seawall—
The ocean said it was hers.

Mink skitters along the rock wall,
startling the dog.

Standing atop the seawall, how many fish
have looked up at me looking down at them?

How many fish have seen me
tossing wish rocks from my porch into the sea?

Lunicurrent

Close the shade of wondering,
lock tight curiosity's salty air,
 brush away rain,
but leave the door ajar.

For love always wanders at night,
unable to sleep
to the melody of that unmissable breath—
the sound of whales.

Standing on my porch
in the dark, staring into
 the ink black ocean,
instinct tells me to break this locked-in gaze,
just turn and go back inside my cabin,
back to the cave of warm covers.

But here, there is a wildness
 walking the beach,
and if I tilt my head just right,
I can hear her wet footsteps,
I can feel her hand still on my shoulder.

Local Geology

For Maleah

Strike slip faults, granite plutons and
      heatstone cairns—A friend needed new windows,

she said, and so she tossed rocks into the plate glass.
      Every spring, rocks fall from logged hillsides,

blocking our way to and from town. And on those
      same bluffs, guardrails have never stopped us

from going over if we really wanted. What does it matter
      if it's simply our glacial erratics,

or something worse? —Our historical record is skewed.

The bones of our stories have long ago slipped
      across our terrains. Sometimes, we recall them

while driving past the old cemetery. Something
      shudders our foothold—a marble headstone

covered in moss, the scent of a City Park fire.
      It was as if it was yesterday, a cousin body-slammed

a bedroom door off its hinges to get to his wife,
      and some new cop played a clicking game

with a gun's muzzle against his wife's head.
      These are our foundations, our driveways,

our dirt roads—our island's groundwork is built on this.
      And I've returned after twenty years—Gravel

is strewn across the highway after the same storms.
      There are occasional earthquakes.

The land is hungry. It can open up at any moment
 and swallow us. There is no

women's shelter here—so we must still speak in stones.

Storm at Mickey's Fishcamp

Praise to the dark windowpane, slant light,
a mournful echo of midnight.

Praise to songs of ancient pines, stitch-thin grass
swaying in porch glow.

Praise to those who sleep sound, but especially
those who wander outside like me,

socks wet from decking, sweater clutched tight,
our ancestors' memories sharp beneath skin.

Praise to sea witches, serpents, the lurking,
the sleek, wet, knobby, the big round-eyed,

water breathers, and air suckers. Praise to the known,
and unknown, the near and beyond,

the breath I draw in and hold tight, the sigh
exhaled, drowned by wind.

Praise to conjuring storm, somewhere knots untied.
Praise to splash and jangle, clank,

and bend and wobble enfolding me. Praise to heron's squawk
bruising a path down my spine.

Praise to this storm, seawall beneath my feet,
five fingers clutching porch rail,
a white plastic chair bobbing in the waves.

Retroflection

Press palm to sea, work the ocean,
    flatten it into a mirror

reflecting the Old Woman's light back to you.
    She is Ocean,

who wants what she wants—You've known this
    your whole life. She wants your body,

your cousins' body, your uncle's body,
    anyone's body. All these drownings

in your family history too numerous to speak of.
    She considers them gifts.

See her as she really is—Ocean simply wants
    her broken coral ribs mended, her sea hair

combed and braided, a caretaking as old
    as stories carved on cave walls,

and etched in stone on a nearby beach.
    After all, don't you recall her retroflection—

a current turning back on itself,
    how her hand reached up to yours,

in Brown Bear Bay, how you leaned over
    the boat's gunwales—there you are/were

with your fingertips swirling through
    flashing green diatoms, resisting

the urge to jump in, swim in her liquid light,
    while above you, a meteor

left a silver trail across August's black sky.

From the Body that is an Ocean

Some days I feel like I surround continents
        and churn a kaleidoscope of currents
on a mapmaker's chart.

I flip up krill and wash over kelp beds.
        Like me, you've begun in water.
But I remember everything,

the sharp-tuned heartbeat,
        voices gathering outside our tent wall.
I am not surprised by this knowing, still.

The slope of shore to tideline,
        I walk every day is my escape. Moments
stolen from this unhinged world.

Here at the edge of the edge, everything is enormous.
        Some days the ocean is like silk,
somedays there are shadows beneath

the gray cloud's downcast gaze. These days,
        I remind myself it's enough
just to consider the water-strider,

in the stagnant stream beside my cabin
        who never considers puddle or ocean,
with her groves of leg hairs trapping air,

        walking atop her sea,
water-skipping toward the fallen dragonfly.

Acknowledgements

Alaska Women Speak: "Fishcamp Kismet," "The Driving Force," and "Storm at Mickey's Fishcamp"
Plant Human Quarterly: "Foraging Zone"
Terrain Magazine: "Retroflection"
The Dodge: "Seawall"
Tidal Echoes: "Reference Station," "Overlooking," "Map of Dogs," "Local Geology," "Kymatology," and "Cabin Aubade"

About the Author

Vivian Faith Prescott was born and raised on the small island of Wrangell, Kaachxana.áak'w, in Southeast Alaska on the land of the Shtax'heen Kwáan. She lives and writes in Lingít Aaní at her family's fishcamp. She is a member of the Pacific Sámi Searvi and a founding member of the first LGBTQIA group on the island. She's the author of several poetry collections and works of non-fiction and fiction. Along with her daughter, Vivian Mork Yéilk', she co-hosts the award-winning *Planet Alaska* Facebook page and co-authors the *Planet Alaska* column appearing in the Juneau Empire.

Glass Lyre Press

exceptional works to replenish the spirit

Glass Lyre Press is an independent literary publisher interested in technically accomplished, stylistically distinct, and original work. Glass Lyre seeks diverse writers that possess a dynamic aesthetic and an ability to emotionally and intellectually engage a wide audience of readers.

Glass Lyre's vision is to connect the world through language and art. We hope to expand the scope of poetry and short fiction for the general reader through exceptionally well-written books, which evoke emotion, provide insight, and resonate with the human spirit.

Poetry Collections
Poetry Chapbooks
Select Short & Flash Fiction
Anthologies

www.GlassLyrePress.com

www.ingramcontent.com/pod-product-compliance
Lightning Source LLC
LaVergne TN
LVHW041640070526
838199LV00052B/3470